A Gift From

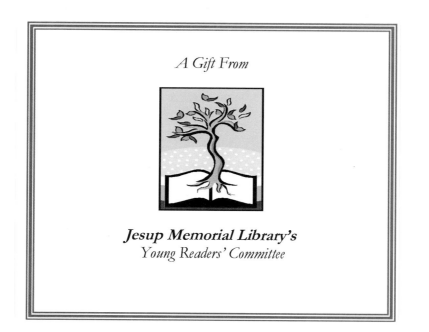

Jesup Memorial Library's
Young Readers' Committee

KINGDOM CLASSIFICATION

COCCI, SPIRILLA & OTHER
BACTERIA

By Steve Parker

First published in the United States in 2009 by
Compass Point Books
151 Good Counsel Drive
P.O. Box 669
Mankato, MN 56002-0669

KINGDOM CLASSIFICATION—BACTERIA
was produced by

David West Children's Books
7 Princeton Court
55 Felsham Road
London SW15 1AZ

This book was manufactured with paper containing
at least 10 percent post-consumer waste.

Designer: Rob Shone
Editors: Gail Bushnell, Anthony Wacholtz
Page Production: Bobbie Nuytten

Art Director: LuAnn Ascheman-Adams
Creative Director: Joe Ewest
Editorial Director: Nick Healy
Managing Editor: Catherine Neitge

Library of Congress Cataloging-in-Publication Data
Parker, Steve, 1952–
   Cocci, spirilla & other bacteria / by Steve Parker.
      p. cm.—(Kingdom classifications)
   Includes index.
   ISBN 978-0-7565-4225-2 (library binding)
   1. Bacteria—Juvenile literature.
I. Title. II. Title: Cocci, spirilla and other bacteria.
III. Series: Parker, Steve, 1952– Kingdom
classifications.
   QR74.8.P37 2009
   572.8'293—dc22   2009007524

Visit Compass Point Books on the Internet at
www.compasspointbooks.com
or e-mail your request to
custserv@compasspointbooks.com

PHOTO CREDITS :
Abbreviations: t-top, m-middle, b-bottom, r-right,
l-left, c-center.

Cover, 6–7, 10b, ARS/USDA/Eric Erbe; 3, 4–5, 17bl, 17br, 27t,
38–39b, 40t, 41ml, 45br, CDC/Janice Carr; 8t, Wikimedia/
HolgerK; 8mt, Andrew Dunn; 8mb, Jan van der Crabben; 8–9,
25mr, 33b, NASA; 9c, Wikimedia/Felix Andrews; 9mtr, CDC/
Courtesy of Larry Stauffer, Oregon State Public Health
Laboratory; 9mbr, 20m, Wikimedia/Christian Fischer; 9bl, Jim
Peaco/NPS; 9br, Department of Microbiology, University of
Hawaii at Manoa; 11mr, 31bl, 31br, 34–35, 40–41, 41mr, 43t,
CDC; 12l, Tina Carvalho/University of Hawaii, Original image
courtesy of Rocky Mountain Laboratories, NIAID, NIH;
12–13t, 18br, 20t, 26–27, 28b, 28–29, OSF/Dennis Kunkel; 13tr,
13m, 39b, Tina Carvalho/University of Hawaii; 13br, WHO;
14l, Wikimedea/Paul Harrison; 14r, Corbis Royalty Free; 15mr,
Ernest Orlando; 15bl, OSF/James Dennis; 15br, CDC/Dr. Barry
S. Fields; 16bl, ARS/USDA/De Wood; 16–17, CDC/Elizabeth H.
White, M.S.; 17mr, Trance Gemini; 18t, ARS/USDA/Scott Bauer;
18bl, ARS/USDA; 19tl, Dr. Bob Embley, NOAA PMEL; 19tr,
iStockphoto/David Parsons; 19ml, Wikimedia/Roger Griffith;
19c, Eleanor Robbins, USGS; 19b, NOAA; 20–21, Jialiang Gao;
21t, Wikimedia/Øystein Paulsen; 21mr, Wikimedia/William K. Li
and Frédéric Partensky, Bedford Institute of Oceanography;
21br, Ocean Explorer/NOAA; 22b, Andrew King & Pete
Davison/Barbeau Lab; 22–23, Wikimedia/Hans Hillewaert; 23t,
Gerald Allen; 23m, Prof. J.W. Hastings; 23ml, 23bl, Paw
Dalgaard, Ph.D.; 24l, iStockphoto/Steve Rabin; 24m, Wikimedia/
Mila Zinkova; 24bl, Richard B. Hoover, Elena Pikuta and Asim
Bej, NASA/NSSTC University of Alabama at Huntsville, and the
University of Alabama at Birmingham; 25t, Jim Pisarowicz/NPS;
25ml, Wikimedia/Oak Ridge National Laboratory; 25c, NASA/
JPL/USGS; 25b, NOAA/C. Van Dover/OAR/NURP/College of
William & Mary; 26t, Prof. Dag O. Hessen, University of Oslo;
26bl, 26br, Jeffrey M. Vinocur; 29c, OSF/Gopal Murti; 30b,
iStockphoto/Oleg Sviridov; 30mr, Wikimedia/Eric Moody; 31t,
31m, 34b, 35m, 38–39t, 43m, CDC/James Gathany; 32bl,
Matthias Kabel; 32br, Wikimedia/Rainer Zenz; 32–33, OSF/Dr.
Gary D. Gaugler; 33t, iStockphoto/Dave White; 33mr,
iStockphoto/Ewen Cameron; 34m, Los Alamos National
Laboratory/Kevin N. Roark; 35t, OSF/Maximilian Stock Ltd;
35b, iStockphoto/Rade Pavlovic; 36b, Wikimedia/Arthur
Friedlander/NIAID; 36–37, Wikimedia/Rocky Mountain
Laboratories, NIAID, NIH; 37tl, Wikimedia/Rocky Mountain
Laboratories, NIAID, NIH; 37tr, iStockphoto/Willie B. Thomas;
37mr, W-L. Deng and A. Collmer, Cornell University, Ithaca,
N.Y.; 37bl, Wikimedia/Kevin Walsh; 37br, Thomas A. Zitter,
Cornell University, Ithaca, N.Y.; 38bl, iStockphoto/
mammamaart; 39tr, OSF/James Cavallini; 39ml, Wikimedia/Bob
Metcalf; 39mr, Yutaka Tsutsumi, M.D. Prof., Department of
Pathology Fujita Health University School of Medicine; 40b,
iStockphoto/Andrei Malov; 41tl, 41tr, Wikimedia/U.S.
Departement of Health and Human Services; 41b, DoD photo
by Petty Officer 3rd Class Mike Larson, U.S. Navy; 42l, NCBI/
Dr. Hans Ackermann; 43b, Wikimedia/Dr. Al Jenny/USDA.

Front cover: Escherichia coli
Opposite: Unidentified bacterial biofilm

COCCI, SPIRILLA & OTHER
BACTERIA

Steve Parker

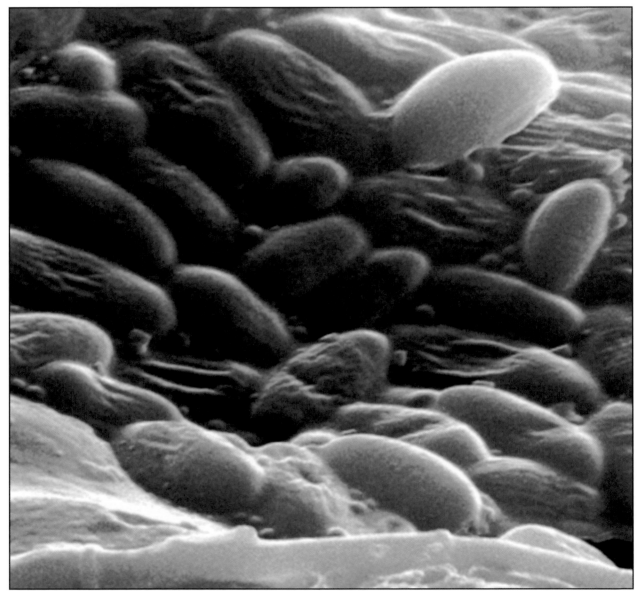

Compass Point Books ✦ Minneapolis, Minnesota

TABLE OF CONTENTS

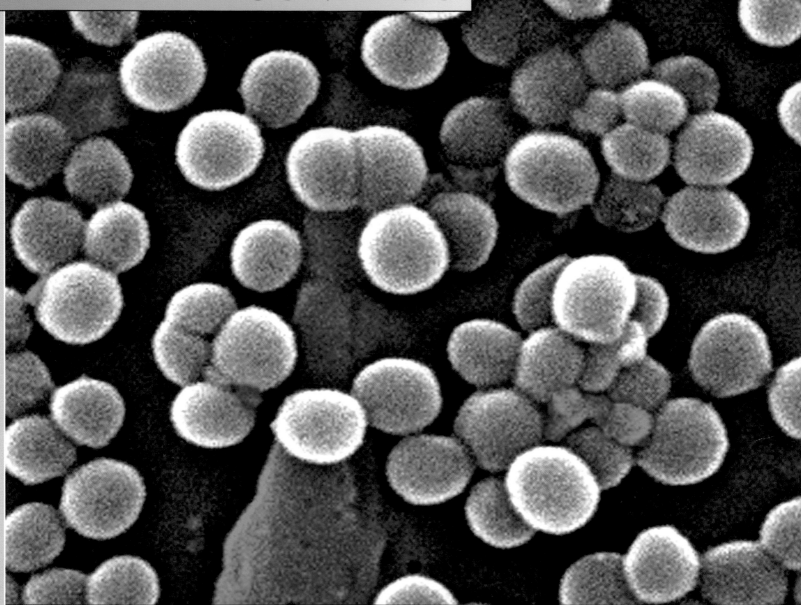

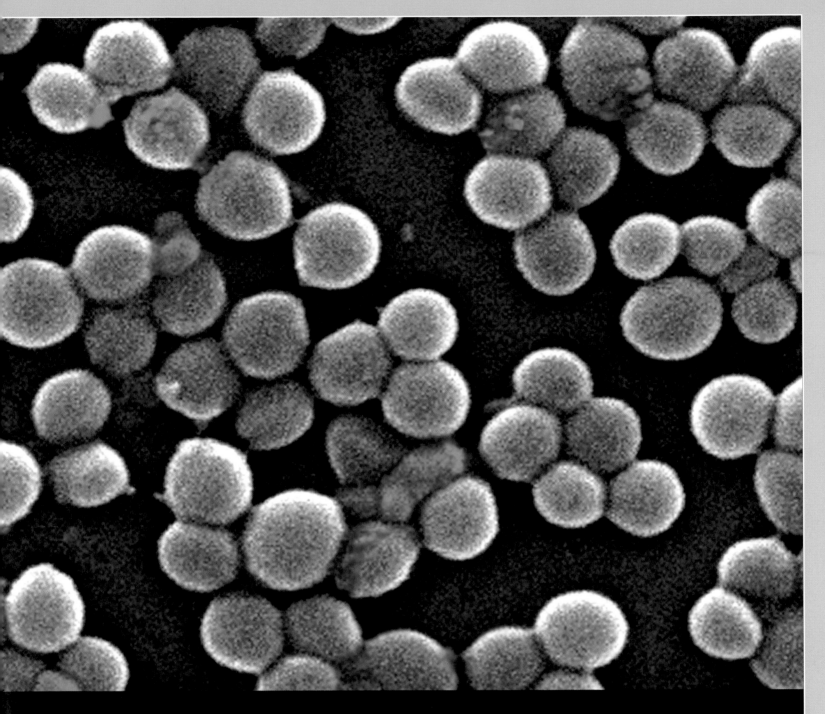

It's all around us—in the air, soil, and water, in our homes and buildings, in cars, trains, ships, and planes, and in every dark corner you can imagine. Yet we cannot see it. The microscopic world is everywhere, but it is strange and unfamiliar. It's home to living things that are so unusual and different from bigger animals and plants that they could be mistaken for aliens from another planet. Many of these creatures are bacteria—the most common and widespread life-forms on Earth.

Bacteria are known by a variety of common names, such as microbes, germs, and bugs. They are much too small to see without a microscope. If you shrank a huge stadium full of 100,000 people down to the size of this "o," the people would then be as small as bacteria. But although bacteria are so small, they are vitally important. Bacteria help plants to grow, assist animals in digesting their food, rot away dead bodies, are used to make medicines, and much more.

FROM THE MICRO-WORLD

The best-known bacterium (plural: bacteria) is Escherichia coli, *a name usually shortened to E. coli. It lives in many places, from the soil to inside the human body. E. coli are usually shaped like sausages. A string of 12,500 of them in a row would stretch about $^{3}/8$ inch (1 centimeter). There are many strains, or kinds, of E. coli. "Good" strains live inside our intestines, where billions of them help to process the food we eat. But "bad" strains of E. coli can cause serious illness.*

BACTERIA EVERYWHERE

No one knows how many species of bacteria there are. The harder we search, the more species we find. The total number may be much more than 10 million. But we do know that bacteria live almost everywhere we look.

AMAZING NUMBERS

In the late 1970s, the scientists who specialize in the study of bacteria, known as bacteriologists, estimated around 10,000 to 20,000 species of bacteria. But new methods of identifying them, especially by using their genetic material, show that the true number of bacterial species could be anywhere between 10 million and 1 billion.

COMPOST Bacillus

BACTERIA ALL AROUND

For many years, scientists knew that bacteria live by the trillions in ponds, rivers, soil, and the decaying bodies of plants and animals. Then they discovered that bacteria thrive inside living animals and plants, too. They still thought some places on Earth were too extreme for bacteria, such as the boiling water of hot springs, the undersides of glaciers and icebergs, and the oozing mud at the cold, black bottom of the deep sea. With better scientific equipment and techniques, we now know that bacteria thrive in all these places and more.

MARSHLAND Alcaligenes

POLAR REGIONS Chryseobacterium

ANIMALS Bacteroides

PONDS Cyanobacteria

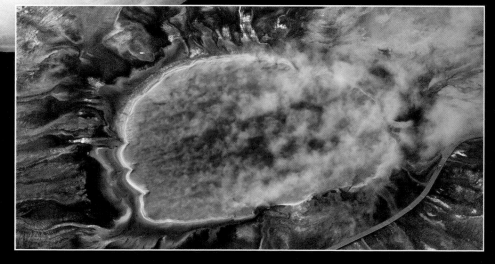

HOT SPRINGS Rhodothermus

MAIN BACTERIA GROUPS

Bacteria were once included in the Monera kingdom. The newer system for classifying life places bacteria in two of the three domains, or groups, of all living things. Domain Bacteria contains "ordinary" types, such as *Streptococcus* and *Bacillus*, plus the cyanobacteria, sometimes called blue-green algae. Domain Archaea includes bacteria such as *Halobacterium*. These bacteria live in extreme conditions such as salt lakes.

Bacillus cereus

Cyanobacteria

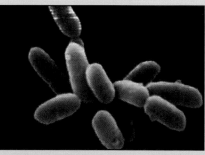

Halobacterium

9

INSIDE A BACTERIUM

Bacteria are very tiny, but they are not particularly simple. Each bacterium is a single living cell. Bacteria have hundreds of even smaller parts, each with its own role or task.

LIFE INSTRUCTIONS

All life-forms have genetic material called DNA. In a bacterium, the DNA floats freely in the cell. In other living things, the DNA is contained in a baglike wrapping called the nuclear membrane. This is a basic difference between bacteria, known as prokaryotes, and other living things, the eukaryotes.

UNDER THE MICROSCOPE

Bacteria are microbes, so you need a microscope to see them. A scanning electron microscope provides a three-dimensional view of bacteria.

DNA

DNA, deoxyribonucleic acid, carries genes, or the instructions for life. It looks like a long, looped thread floating in the cytoplasm.

RIBOSOME

Small blobs called ribosomes use instructions from the genetic material to build the bacterium's various parts from substances called proteins.

PILUS

Some bacteria have tiny hairlike projections called pili sticking out from the capsule. These connect to other bacteria for reproduction.

VACUOLE

Pools of fluid in the cytoplasm contain substances such as water, nutrients, or waste products for removal.

MEMBRANES OR NOT?

Prokaryotes have a flexible cell membrane, or outer "skin," but no separate membranes inside the cell. Eukaryotes do have membranes inside, enclosing structures such as DNA in the nucleus. Eukaryotic cells include single-celled protists such as amoebas and the cells of animals and plants.

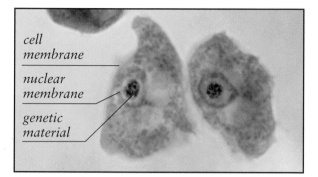

cell membrane

nuclear membrane

genetic material

Eukaryotes carry genes in the nucleus.

CAPSULE

The bacterium's outermost layer is the capsule. It is a strong, tough container that protects the delicate parts inside.

CELL WALL

The cell wall gives the bacterium its shape. It is made from "building blocks" of peptidoglycan, which is not found in the cell walls of plants or animals.

CELL MEMBRANE

This flexible layer is a selective barrier that lets in useful substances, such as nutrients, but keeps out harmful ones.

PLASMID

Apart from the main section of DNA, bacteria also have strings or loops of genetic material called plasmids. They carry instructions that are useful for survival in certain conditions.

FLAGELLUM

Some bacteria have long, whiplike flagella. These swish or spin around to make the bacterium move along in water.

Bacteria grow in almost every kind of shape, from balls and rods to boxes, corkscrews, and stars. And even though they are all small, the biggest bacteria are hundreds of times larger than the smallest ones.

SPHERICAL IN NATURE

The Streptococcus *group of bacteria are mostly spherical or ball-like. They tend to grow joined together as long chains like necklaces. Some types of* Streptococcus *cause the throat to become red and sore, a disease known as strep throat.*

ALL ABOUT SIZE

The biggest known bacterium was discovered in mud from the seabed near Namibia in 1999. Named *Thiomargarista*, it measures up to about 1/32 of an inch (0.75 millimeters) across. Most bacteria are about 1/25000 to 1/5000 of an inch (0.001 to 0.005 mm) long. The tiniest, such as *Mycoplasma*, are one-tenth this size.

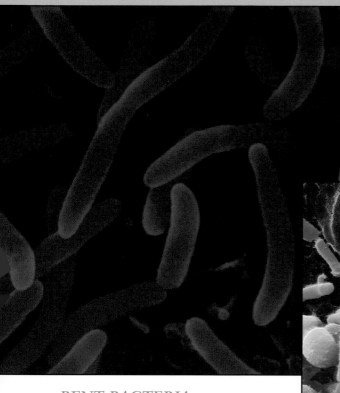

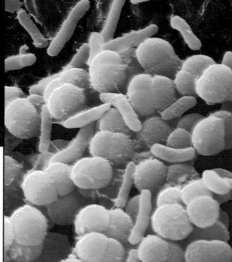

BENT BACTERIA

The bacteria known as Vibrios are mostly bent sticks or rods. They can also be shaped like a comma. Some types can live without oxygen.

SCREW-SHAPED

Bacteria with a corkscrew shape, known as a helix, are in the spirochaete group. They spin and twirl as they move.

UNDER THE SCOPE

Most of the differently shaped groups of bacteria can be identified under a high-power light microscope. Each group has its own features. For example, the *Vibrios* and spirochaetes can live without oxygen, which is essential for other kinds of living things. These bacteria thrive in stale, unmoving water and mud.

PAIRS AND CLUMPS

Rodlike bacteria are bacilli. Cocci are separate balls, while diplococci are balls joined as pairs. Staphylococci are clumps of balls.

SEEING BACTERIA

The largest known bacteria are visible as tiny specks to the unaided eye. The smallest are too tiny to see clearly under a light microscope. Other types of microscopes are needed, like the electron microscope, which sends out beams of electrons (the smallest particles inside atoms).

If the largest bacterium was magnified 10 million times, it would be as big as an elephant. Then an ordinary bacterium would be the size of a honey bee, while the smallest would be as tiny as a flea.

13

STONY LUMPS
In some warm shallow seas, such as Shark Bay in Australia, lumps of "stone" grow slowly. Known as stromatolites, they are made by algae and bacteria. Fossil stromatolites are more than 3 billion years old.

When Earth began almost 4.6 billion years ago, there was no life. By 3.5 billion years ago, the planet had cooled and oceans formed. In them appeared early living things—bacteria.

FROM THE START
At first Earth was a dangerous, fiery place with red-hot rocks, volcanoes, and earthquakes. No life could survive. It took more than 500 million years for the earliest life-forms to appear.

MICRO-FOSSILS
Scientists believe the earliest living things were similar to bacteria of today. Part of the evidence is microscopic fossils—remains of once-living things preserved in rocks and turned to stone. Rocks more than 3 billion years old contain dotlike fossils, probably of bacteria and similar early life-forms.

CHANGING THE EARTH
The atmosphere (air) of early Earth contained gases such as methane, which is poisonous to animals. As early bacteria lived and died in the oceans over millions of years, they produced other gases—including oxygen. Oxygen levels gradually rose, and the poisonous gases decreased, allowing plants and animals to evolve.

INVADERS

As bigger plants and animals appeared, some bacteria may have gotten inside their cells. These invading bacteria eventually became permanent parts of the cells, such as mitochondria and chloroplasts.

MITOCHONDRIA

Sausage-shaped mitochondria inside the cells of animals and plants are about the same size as bacteria. They are "energy factories," breaking apart food nutrients to release energy for the cell's life processes.

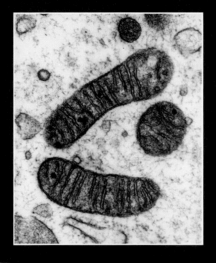

MAGNETIC BACTERIA

The bacterium called *Magnetospirillum* builds up tiny particles inside of magnetic, iron-based minerals. This makes the bacterium work like a miniature bar magnet or compass needle. It swings around to line up with Earth's natural north-south magnetic field. If a stronger, man-made magnet is brought near, the bacteria move to line up with the bar magnet. How these bacteria became magnetic is a mystery.

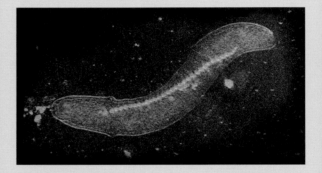

Magnetospirillum *was discovered in 1975.*

LIVING TOGETHER

With its pseudopodium, or long tentacle, an amoeba (pink) captures a bacterium (green) to eat. Millions of years ago, bacteria may have survived this and become useful partners inside the bigger cells, a relationship known as symbiosis.

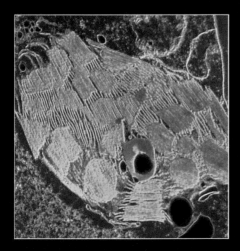

CHLOROPLASTS

Many plant cells contain chloroplasts—tiny structures that look like stacks of sheets. They capture the sun's light energy and change it into sugars, which the plant uses as food. Chloroplasts may have started as bacteria entering plant cells.

HOW BACTERIA MOVE

Some bacteria cannot move under their own power. They drift in water or float in air. But others move quite fast in water, using various parts, such as long, hairlike flagella. These turn and rotate using a system that is nature's equivalent of our own useful invention, the spinning motor.

MOVING AROUND

Why do bacteria need to move? There are various reasons. Some bacteria can detect tiny amounts of food substances. As they wander around, they detect where the food is more abundant and head in that direction. Other bacteria are harmed by certain substances in the surroundings, such as oxygen or methane, so they move away.

ON THE GO

Some E. coli have long, pink flagella pointing in various directions. Bacteria that can move on their own are called motile.

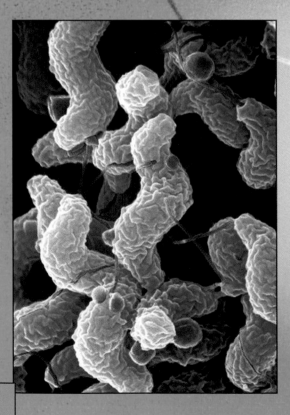

ONE EACH

Each Campylobacter is monotrichous, meaning it has one long flagellum. Scientists have studied this very large flagellum to see how it works.

BACTERIA ARE LIKE MOTORS

The base of a bacterial flagellum is set into the cell membrane. It spins around because of particles called positive ions in the collar-shaped rotor at the base. The positive ions push against negative ions in the stator fixed into the membrane. Some flagella spin around 15 times every second.

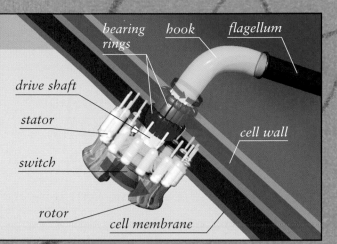

bearing rings · hook · flagellum

drive shaft

stator

switch

rotor

cell membrane

cell wall

MANY FLAGELLA

Some bacteria, such as *Spirillum*, have a tuft of small flagella at one end. Others, like *Proteus*, have small flagella all over, like fur. Each flagellum has a hook at its base next to the bacterium's surface. The hook bends into the "motor" of the flagellum. The motor turns around quickly, making the flagellum swing around. The flagellum itself is a bendable tube that is light but strong.

SLIMING ALONG
Myxobacteria slide along like micro-slugs by gliding on slime. They roam about in groups called wolf packs and sometimes clump together into mushroom shapes to breed.

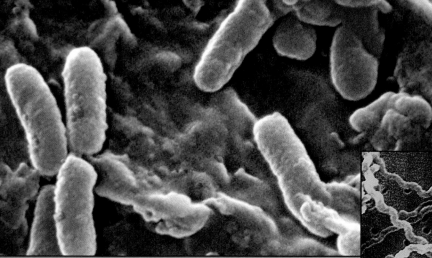

PSEUDOMONAS
Certain strains of Pseudomonas (above) "swim" with one flagellum, and some have two or more. Some live harmlessly in soil, but others cause diseases.

LEPTOSPIRA
Leptospira *(below) has two flagella, one at each end. The flagella wave about in the narrow gap between the cell wall and cell membrane.*

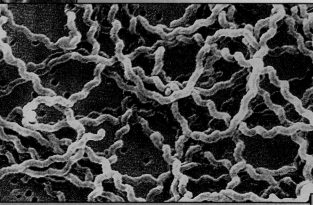

Almost any natural substance in the world is used by certain kinds of bacteria for food. Bacteria even eat some man-made materials.

NEED FOR NITROGEN

Several kinds of bacteria take in nitrogen-containing substances for growth and energy. Some get their nitrogen from the air, where it forms 80 percent of the atmosphere. Some obtain nitrogen when it is dissolved in water in the form of natural minerals known as nitrates and nitrites.

FIXING NITROGEN

Bacteria that take in nitrogen from the air and build it into substances in their own cells are nitrogen "fixers." Some live in root nodules (below) of the pea-and-bean plant family called legumes, like soya (above right). The plant gains nitrogen-rich substances, and the bacteria have a safe living place—an example of the beneficial partnership of symbiosis.

COMMON FIXER
Bradyrhizobium *(below) is one of the most common kinds of nitrogen-fixing bacteria.*

The carbon monoxide gas made by vehicle engines is poisonous to us and other animals. But it's food to the bacteria Pseudomonas carboxydovorans, *which are found in the soil.*

MICROBIAL MATS

Some bacteria and other microscopic life-forms, such as algae, grow in thick layers called mats (left). They may make a hard cover from stony minerals for protection and to keep warm.

IRON-EATERS

Gallionella *bacteria (below right) use iron-containing substances as food. As they "eat," they add oxygen to the iron to form iron oxide, or rust. This may stain the surroundings brown (below).*

GAINING ENERGY

The substance sulfur, in the form of dissolved sulfates or sulfides, is a favorite food of certain bacteria. As with nitrogen, the bacteria take in tiny molecules of these minerals through pores, or holes, in their cell wall and membrane. Once inside, these molecules—groups of atoms—are rearranged to release the energy that held the atoms together. The bacteria then use the energy for their life processes, such as growth, movement, and waste disposal.

RUSTICLES

Many sunken wrecks of iron or steel ships slowly become decorated by amazing shapes, like icicles or lacy cloth. These are known as rusticles. They are formed by chemotrophic bacteria—those that feed on chemicals.

Iron rusticles on the wreck of the Titanic.

GROWING WITH LIGHT

Plants grow by a process called photosynthesis. They capture light energy from the sun to make energy-rich substances, which they use as food for growth and survival. Certain kinds of bacteria, known as photosynthetic bacteria, can do the same.

THYLAKOIDS

Green plants have tiny, free-floating parts called chloroplasts in their cells. Chloroplasts help carry out photosynthesis. Cyanobacteria (top) are mostly greenish or blue-tinged and live in colonies (above). They have multi-sheet structures called thylakoids made from the main cell membrane. Photosynthesis happens on the surfaces.

CYANOBACTERIA

The main group of bacteria that carries out photosynthesis is cyanobacteria, also called blue-green algae. (They are not true algae, which are more like simple plants.) As in green plants, cyanobacteria take in carbon dioxide and add it to water using light energy. This makes sugars and other high-energy foods. The process also makes oxygen, which we and other animals breathe to stay alive. Cyanobacteria live in the oceans, in fresh water, and in damp places on land.

GREEN AND PURPLE

Many other types of bacteria capture light energy. They include green bacteria, such as *Chlorobium* in the sea, and the heliobacteria of waterlogged mud and soil. Another group is the purple bacteria, such as *Rhodospirillum*, which are found in shallow, sandy seas and mudflats. All of these bacteria are photo-trophic, which means they use light to grow. Tiny and numerous, they are eaten by slightly larger living things, such as protists and tiny animals. These are then eaten by bigger animals, and so on, building up the food webs of nature.

SMALL TO BIG

Shrimplike creatures called krill are part of food chains that begin with light-capturing bacteria in the sea and end with the biggest animals—great whales.

MUD LOVERS

Heliobacteria such as Heliobacter (left) do not like too much oxygen or being exposed to air. They flourish in the mud of flooded fields known as paddies where rice grows (below).

SECRETS OF THE SARGASSO

Prochlorococcus is one of the smallest photosynthetic bacteria. It is also one of the most numerous living things on Earth, with 100,000 in a single drop of seawater. Discovered in the Sargasso Sea in 1986, it makes one-fifth of all the oxygen in Earth's atmosphere.

Prochlorococcus (above, right) was first identified in the Sargasso Sea of the North Atlantic (above).

GLOW-IN-THE-DARK BACTERIA

The ability of living things to give out light is known as bioluminescence. In the oceans are bioluminescent fish, squid, jellyfish, clams, worms, and other creatures. But it's not the actual animals that glow—it's their bacteria.

PRODUCING LIGHT

The tiny bacteria in these glowing sea creatures make light by changing energy in chemical substances into light energy. (This is the opposite of photosynthesis.) The chemical luciferase adds oxygen to another substance, causing a brief flash of light. This happens thousands of times per second to produce a continuous glow.

LOOSEJAW FISH

Light-making bacteria are usually in groups in their host known as photophores. The loosejaw has a red photophore under the eye and a green one behind it.

CAMOUFLAGE

The bobtail squid or little cuttlefish of the Atlantic Ocean has light-making organs. Many are in the mantle—its fleshy, cloaklike body covering. It contains the bacteria Vibrio fischeri, which produce the correct amount of light to camouflage the squid in various lighting conditions.

WHY SHINE?

Why do so many sea creatures shine in the gloom? Some are looking for breeding partners in the ocean's vast darkness. The pattern of lights shows whether the other animal is one of their own kind. Some attract smaller animals that are curious about the light. They come too close and get eaten. Some flash briefly when in danger, then turn off and escape into the blackness.

FLASHLIGHT FISH

A bioluminescent creature gives its bacteria a safe home while using the light to help it survive. But the bacteria cannot be switched on and off easily. The flashlight fish has flaps of skin to move over its lights to "flash" them on and off.

The flashing lights of a flashlight fish are under the eyes.

MAKING LIGHT WORK

Common types of glowing bacteria include several kinds of Vibrio, also known as Photobacterium. *Different strains make light of differing colors, from yellow to blue (left).*

BACTERIAL ART

Bioglyphs are patterns, drawings, and writing made from glowing bacteria grown on flat trays of jellylike food. They shine in various colors.

SUSPECT SHELLFISH

Shrimp, prawn, and other shellfish can suffer from bacterial diseases, and people who eat them become ill. Some of these bacteria are bioluminescent and can be detected by turning off the light.

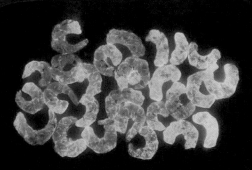

EXTREME LIVING

No other living things on Earth can survive in the harsh and hostile places where some bacteria live. In very low temperatures, places without water, under incredible pressure—bacteria can survive.

EXTREMOPHILES

The general name for living things that endure severe conditions is extremophiles. There are many kinds of extremophile bacteria. Halophiles grow in the saltiest lakes. Acidophiles survive in acidic soils, such as peat swamps. Xerophiles live with almost no water in the driest deserts. Cryophiles persist in intense cold, such as in ice, and thermophiles live in water even hotter than its boiling temperature.

SUPERHOT BATH

The water blasting from Castle Geyser in Yellowstone National Park reaches temperatures of more than 200 degrees Fahrenheit (90 degrees Celsius). Yet thermophilic bacteria thrive there, forming colorful microbial mats around the edges of the water.

SALTY HABITAT

Mono Lake in California (above) is so salty and alkaline—the opposite of acidic—that it has no fish. Only specialized extremophiles live here, such as the bacterium Spirochaeta americana *(right, with living cells, green, and dead cells, red).*

SURVIVAL STRATEGIES

Many extremophile bacteria are from the domain Archaea. They are sometimes known as archaeons rather than bacteria. They have unusual chemical processes inside their cells that are not disrupted by the conditions around them. If the surroundings become even more extreme, they form tough protective capsules or cases around themselves, stop their life processes, and wait for an improvement.

STRINGS OF SLIME

"Snottites" are slimy strings of bacteria hanging from cave ceilings and walls. They feed on the sulfur-rich, acidic chemicals in water trickling through the rocks.

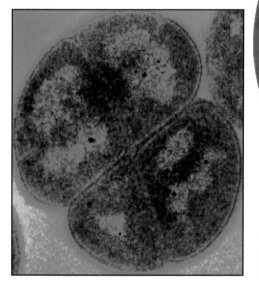

CONAN THE BACTERIUM

The movie Conan the Barbarian *featured a tough warrior from ancient times. "Conan the Bacterium" is the nickname of* Deinococcus radiodurans, *which can handle cold, acids, a lack of water, and even dangerous radioactivity.*

ALIEN LIFE?

Conditions on planets such as Mars are certainly extreme. But it's possible that bacteria or other small, tough life-forms live there, perhaps in the polar ice (above left). A meteorite rock from Mars has wormlike shapes that could be fossilized bacteria (above right).

IN THE DEEP, DARK SEA

At certain places on the ocean floor, jets of hot, mineral-rich water squirt through cracks known as hydrothermal vents. Strange creatures live here, including blind white fish, crabs, and tubeworms that are 6½ feet (2 meters) long. Bacteria inside the worms feed on the minerals in the water and share their nourishment with the worms.

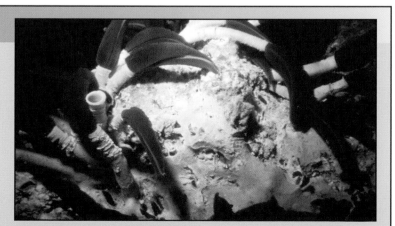

Deep-sea vent tubeworms are as thick as a human arm.

HOW BACTERIA MULTIPLY

Bacteria, like many other microbes, multiply by dividing. Their numbers increase when each bacterium splits into two. The two grow to full size, divide again, and so on.

ONE MAKES TWO

The process of splitting in two to multiply is known as binary fission. First the bacterium copies its genetic material—the full set of DNA, known as its genome. Then its cell wall and membrane tighten or pinch around the middle like a tight belt. Each set of genetic material goes to one end of the cell. The pinching continues until the bacterium looks like a figure eight and finally splits into two separate cells.

NONSTOP CULTURE

In the laboratory, a chemostat machine constantly adds nutrients to bacteria in a liquid and removes wastes and dead cells. The bacteria could keep multiplying forever.

COUNTING BACTERIA

Scientists often need to count bacteria, especially for medical research. The bacteria are put in glass or plastic chambers (above left) and light sensors detect them passing over a grid of squares (left).

ONE TO THREE

As a bacterium splits in two, one offspring may already be dividing again. This happens with Ralstonia, which causes plant diseases.

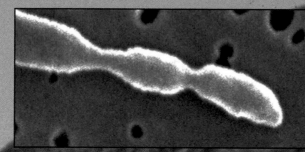

FAST BREEDERS

Most bacteria multiply quickly by binary fission when conditions such as food availability and temperature are good. After dividing, each takes in nourishment and grows back to normal size. Some bacteria can divide every 15 to 20 minutes. One bacterium produces 16 in one hour and 1 million after five hours. If conditions worsen, the bacteria multiply more slowly or stop.

HALFWAY THROUGH

An E. coli bacterium was colored pink by a laboratory dye or stain and preserved about halfway through its halving process. Each of the offspring cells has an equal share of the parts and substances inside.

MORE AND MORE

Individual bacteria are too small to see with the naked eye. But we can see colonies of them as patches, for example, on rotting fruit. As the colony grows, the patch enlarges, with old, dead bacteria at the center and new ones at the edge.

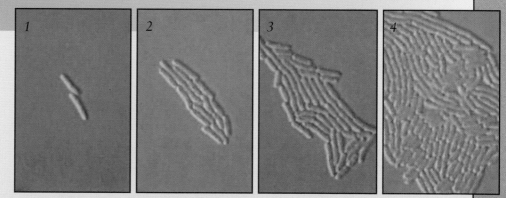

A light microscope view shows Escherichia coli *multiplying after 17 minutes (1), 60 minutes (2), 90 minutes (3), and 150 minutes (4).*

BREEDING BACTERIA

Bacteria divide in half to increase their numbers. They also breed when two or more transfer DNA between themselves to make new combinations of genes.

NEW SETS OF GENES

When a bacterium splits by binary fission, the two offspring have exactly the same genes. When bacteria breed, they come into contact and exchange pieces of DNA carrying various genes. In this way, they gain new combinations of genes that might help their survival in various conditions, such as using a new food source.

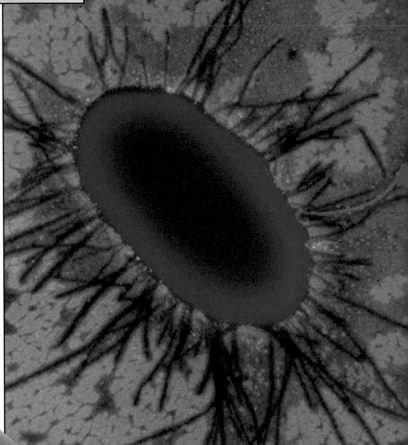

CONJUGATION

Two E. coli bacteria (above) are conjugating—moving genetic material along a tube called the pilus from donor to recipient. The process begins when the recipient detects a chemical called a mating signal produced by the donor.

SPORES

In bad conditions, bacteria such as Clostridium (left) make spores (pink). The tough, thick-walled spores contain just enough genetic material and other parts for survival.

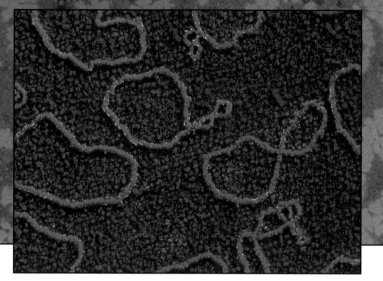

PLASMIDS

The pieces of DNA transferred by breeding bacteria are usually small rings or loops called plasmids. These may be separate from the main section of DNA in the bacterium.

GENE TRANSFER

Many bacteria transfer genes by the process of conjugation. The donor bacterium develops a long tube called the pilus. It moves its pilus so the tip contacts the recipient cell and enters its cell membrane. The donor bacterium then passes a small length of gene-carrying DNA along the pilus and into the recipient. The DNA has already been duplicated, so the donor bacterium still has a copy of it.

TOUGH TIMES

Several kinds of harsh conditions encourage bacteria to breed and form new gene combinations. They might also form tough-walled spores and similar "survival capsules" known as cysts. Such conditions include lack of water, lack of food, and too much heat or cold. Some spores are so tough that they come back to life after being dried out or frozen for hundreds of years.

The driest soil contains billions of bacterial spores.

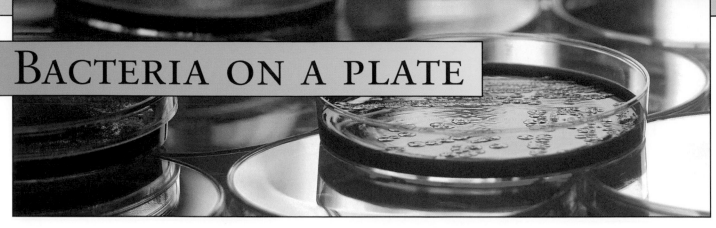

BACTERIA ON A PLATE

I n thousands of laboratories around the world, bacteria are being grown and studied to see how they multiply, breed, and survive.

BACTERIAL CULTURE

Growing bacteria in laboratory equipment is known as culturing. They grow in liquids in flasks or jars. They also grow on jellylike agar gel in trays or in small, round, shallow dishes called petri dishes. The liquid or gel is called the culture medium. It contains nutrients for the bacteria. It may also have other substances such as a test chemical to see whether it is toxic, or poisonous, to the bacteria.

DELICIOUS AGAR

The agar gel used for growing bacteria is warmed to make it runny, mixed with food for the bacteria, and poured into petri dishes to cool. In blood agar (above), the food is blood. Most agar is made from seaweeds such as Gracilaria red seaweed (below). People also use agar in cooking.

BACTERIAL COLONIES

Bacteria are spread onto agar (left) using a wire loop or stick. The bacteria eventually multiply into colonies of millions. The number of colonies and their size are measured regularly.

KEEP IT CLEAN

Bacteria are grown in very strict conditions. Unwanted bacteria float in the air and coat surfaces, so they must be prevented from contaminating the cultured strains. By the same token, dangerous bacteria must be kept in containers or chambers and not allowed to infect people. The laboratory equipment has to be extremely clean. Workers often wear masks, hats, and gowns for protection against harmful bacteria or to keep their own bacteria out of the cultures.

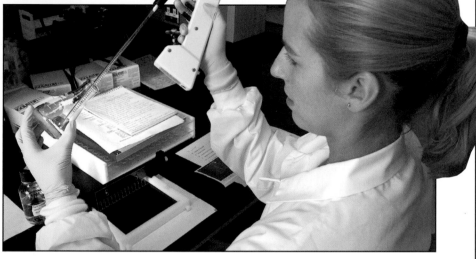

TESTING BACTERIA
After bacteria are grown, they are harvested, or collected, and colored with stains to study under the microscope. Or they are broken apart with chemicals to obtain various substances inside, such as their DNA.

THE GRAM TEST

Bacteria can be dyed with a chemical called the Gram stain. If their outer walls turn purple, they are Gram-positive (G+). If the walls become pink, they are Gram-negative (G-). In general, G- bacteria are more harmful than G+ bacteria, and some cause diseases in people and animals.

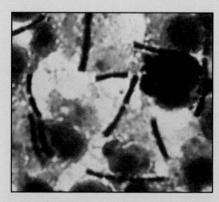

Bacillus anthracis *(G+)*

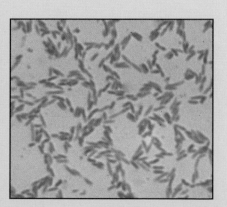

Bacteroides biacutis *(G-)*

USEFUL BACTERIA

A full list of the amazing ways we use bacteria would fill this book. From the age-old art of making cheese to purifying recycled water on the International Space Station, bacteria are our microscopic helpers by the trillion.

FERMENTATION

With the help of bacteria, cheeses and yogurts are made from milk. Particular kinds of bacteria are allowed to grow in the milk and ferment it, using its sugars and other nutrients as food. As the bacteria grow, they make substances that thicken the cheese or yogurt and give it a distinct taste.

MIXING CHEESE

*Certain strains of bacteria produce certain cheeses. Swiss cheese needs three—*Streptococcus thermophilus, Proprionibacter shermani, *and* Lactobacillus.

ACID MAKERS

Lactococcus *is a group of bacteria commonly used for cheeses, crème fraîche, and similar dairy products. As they "eat" the sugars in milk, they make the substance lactic acid, which gives a variety of sharp or sour tastes.*

WORLD OF YOGURTS

Yogurt-type foods of milk fermented by bacteria include cacik *(Turkey, above),* tzatziki *(Greece), and* raita *(India). The milk may be from sheep, goats, horses, or cows.*

VINEGARS

Growing bacteria such as Acetobacter in alcohol ferments it into vinegar (right). The characteristic vinegar taste is caused by ethanoic (acetic) acid produced by the bacteria.

TREATING WASTES

Dirty water from our sinks, bathtubs, and showers, along with human waste from our toilets, goes along drains and sewage pipes to a treatment center. Here a variety of microbes, including many kinds of bacteria, feed on the wastes. In the process, they break down the wastes into simpler, harmless substances and clean the water, which can go back into nature.

PRECIOUS WATER

Clean water is vital in spacecraft and space stations, but it would not be practical to carry fresh water. So water from washing, breathed-out vapor, and urine is cleaned using a variety of filters and membranes. Some of these contain bacteria that break apart unsafe substances into safe ones.

Space engineers test a new bacterial water filter.

SEWAGE SLUDGE

Settling tanks for sewage treatment teem with all kinds of bacteria. They digest the solid wastes that settle on the bottom of the tanks, taking away some of the odor and making them less harmful. The bacteria include Aeromonas, Citrobacter, Bacillus, Escherichia, Micrococcus, and Nitrosomonas.

BACTERIA AND GENES

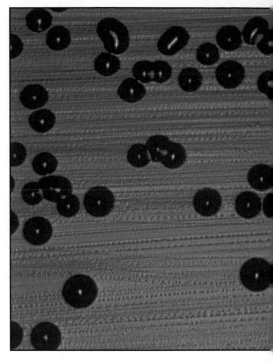

One of the fastest-growing areas of science is genetics. Geneticists study genes to learn how living things develop, carry out their life processes, and breed. Bacteria are vital tools in this high-tech work.

GENOMES

Genes are in the form of long strings of DNA inside living cells. The full set of genes for a particular living thing is known as its genome. Humans have between 20,000 and 25,000 genes. Bacteria are far smaller and simpler, yet some have more than 2,000 genes. These are studied by taking the DNA from bacteria and treating it with chemicals called enzymes to split it into fragments. Other chemicals are added to the fragments to compare their structures.

NUMBER ONE

In 1995 Haemophilus influenzae *was the first organism to have its genome structure worked out. It has about 1,800 genes as one loop of DNA. It got its name because it was once thought to cause influenza (the flu). It was later found that viruses cause the flu.*

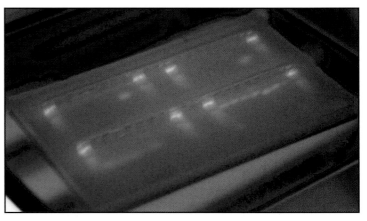

GENETIC BAR CODES

Gel electrophoresis is widely used to study DNA and genes. Fragments of DNA are made to move through a jellylike substance by an electric current. The fragments are then stained to look like dark stripes and compared with known pieces of DNA to identify them.

DNA SEQUENCING

Finding DNA's detailed structure is called sequencing. It detects the order of four substances called bases in the long DNA chain. Just as letters make up words, the order of the bases determines how genes work.

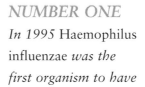

MICRO-FACTORIES

Genetically engineered bacteria grow in large vats called bioreactors. Like billions of microscopic factories, their added genes tell them to make a certain substance, which is taken away and purified for us to use.

NEW COMBINATIONS

The genes of bacteria can be altered. For example, bacteria can use viruses to carry a new gene directly into the bacterial cell. The bacterium then follows the instructions of the new gene, such as making a certain chemical. Bacteria engineered in this way are used to make many products, such as medical drugs.

Polymerase chain reaction is very common in genetics. PCR copies a piece of DNA millions of times to be analyzed in detail using various methods. The copying is done by a chemical called DNA polymerase. The original version of DNA polymerase came from a bacterium—*Thermus aquaticus.*

PCR is widely used to make copies of DNA.

LIFE-SAVING PRODUCT

Genetic engineering involves moving genes from one living thing to another in a process called recombinant DNA technology. An early use of recombinant bacteria was to make insulin, a natural body substance taken using an injection pen (below) by people with diabetes.

Insulin injection

HARMFUL BACTERIA

Not all bacteria are harmful. However, those that are cause many kinds of serious—even deadly—diseases in plants, animals, and people.

PATHOGENS

Living things that cause diseases are known as pathogens. Some kinds of pathogenic bacteria affect both people and animals. They include various types of *Salmonella* and *Bacillus anthracis*, a bacterium that produces anthrax. Anthrax affects the skin, lungs, and intestines. Plants suffer bacterial infections such as cankers, brown spots, and black spots.

ANTHRAX

Rod-shaped anthrax bacteria (below) surround a red blood cell. They are common in soil in the form of tough-cased spores. They get into the body through a skin cut, by being breathed in, or by being eaten.

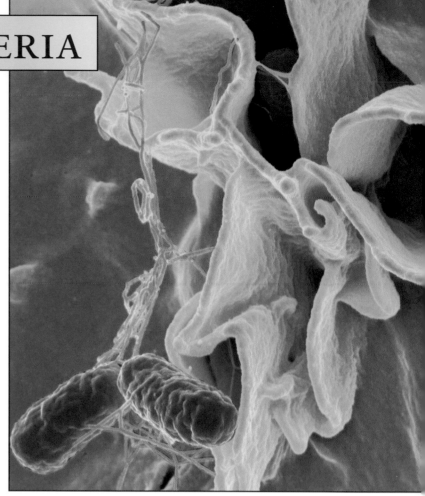

SALMONELLA

There are many strains of Salmonella bacteria (above, red, invading the folded surface of a human cell). They can cause minor digestive upsets or more serious types of food poisoning. Salmonella enterica causes typhoid fever, which kills more than half a million people every year.

BIOWARFARE

The use of harmful bacteria and other germs in biological warfare is banned by worldwide agreement. But it was tried many years ago. The bacteria that cause anthrax, plague, typhoid, and other diseases were grown and put into bombs and other weapons. They were also put into the enemy's water supplies.

PLAGUE

The plague bacterium Yersinia pestis *is spread by the bites of rat fleas. Humans can catch the disease if bitten by the fleas. Through the centuries, the bacterium has caused the Black Death and bubonic plague. It has resulted in the deaths of millions.*

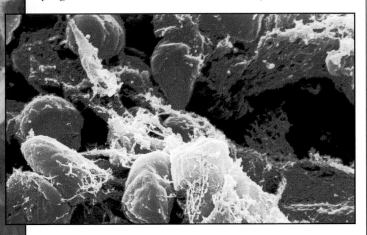

INFECTION

Bacteria can infect a person's body in many ways. They can enter a body when a person breathes, eats or drinks, or has a dirty cut. Once inside, they are warm and have plenty of nutrients, especially in the blood. They multiply fast and spread around the body. Some kinds also produce poisonous waste products called bacterial toxins. The toxin of *Clostridium botulinum*, which causes botulism, is one of the deadliest substances known. A test tube of it could kill millions of people.

Gruinard Island, in West Scotland, was a test site for anthrax germ warfare in the 1940s.

KENNEL COUGH

The coughing, sneezing, and retching of kennel cough is caused by the bacterium Bordetella bronchiseptica. It spreads quickly between dogs kept close together, such as in kennels.

ROTTEN TOMATOES

Certain strains of Pseudomonas bacteria (right, colored green with glowing chemicals) attack plants, including wheat, barley, maple trees, beets, and peas. Often the signs are rotting patches, as in tomato canker (below).

37

HUMAN BACTERIAL DISEASES

If bacteria are all around us, why isn't everyone ill more often? Our bodies have defenses that keep out the bacteria or attack them if they manage to get in. We can also take many precautions to help prevent the spread of bacterial infections.

OUTER DEFENSES

Human skin is usually coated with millions of bacteria that float in the air and land on all surfaces. But our tough skin prevents the bacteria from entering unless it is broken by a cut, sore, or wound. This is why we should always clean cuts and other broken skin quickly and carefully and keep them covered until they heal.

INNER DEFENSES

Bacteria that get through the skin or the delicate linings of the nose, throat, and lungs are attacked by white blood cells. These pale-looking cells move around in the blood and "eat" bacteria and other microbes.

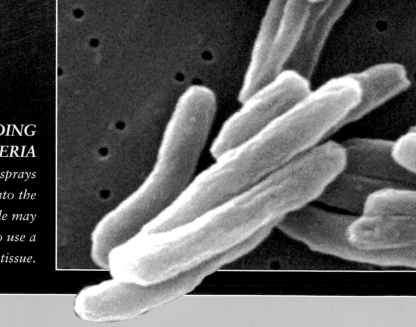

SPREADING BACTERIA

A cough or sneeze sprays thousands of bacteria into the air, which other people may breathe in. It's best to use a handkerchief or tissue.

HANDLE WITH CARE

It's important to wash your hands before and after handling pets and their equipment. For example, turtles can pass Salmonella bacteria to people. It also prevents us from passing infections to our pets.

DIRTY WATER

Millions of people around the world do not have clean, safe drinking water. It teems with Vibrio cholerae bacteria (which causes cholera), typhoid bacteria, and other types.

KEEPING CLEAN

Good cleanliness and hygiene are very important to keep bacteria at bay. You should wash yourself regularly so they don't build up on the skin. You should also wash your hands before touching food. Then bacteria can't transfer onto the food and end up in your stomach.

TUBERCULOSIS

The lung disease tuberculosis is a worldwide killer caused by Mycobacterium tuberculosis. Each year about 2 million people die from it.

NEW FINDS

Scientists continue to find new bacterial diseases. In the 1980s, it was discovered that ulcers—raw patches in the stomach (above)—are usually caused by the bacterium Helicobacter pylori (above right). This led to successful new treatments for ulcers.

GERM THEORY OF DISEASE

Our understanding of which bacteria or other microbes cause which infections is based on the germ theory of disease. It dates back to German doctor and research scientist Robert Koch (1843–1910). He devised a set of rules to prove that a particular bacterium really does cause an illness, rather than it just happening to be in the body at the time. Koch identified the bacteria that cause anthrax, cholera, and tuberculosis.

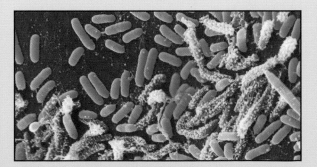

Identifying harmful bacteria is a crucial task.

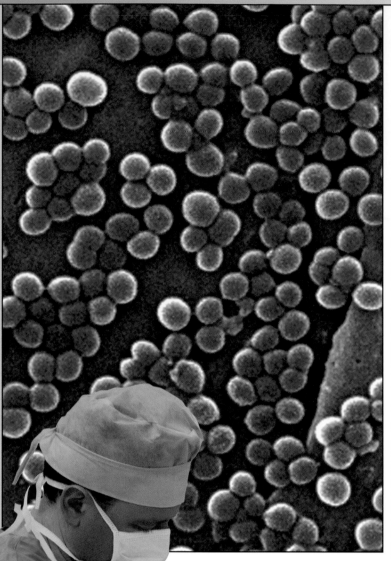

We have many helpers in our war against harmful bacteria and other germs. They include chemicals such as antiseptics and disinfectants, as well as medical drugs known as antibiotics.

ANTIBIOTICS

An antibiotic is a medicine designed to kill bacteria or disable them so that they cannot multiply. The first one discovered was penicillin in 1928. It is made by a natural fungus or mold in the soil. Since then hundreds of antibiotics have been developed to treat many bacterial diseases. Some strains of bacteria, however, can become resistant to or unaffected by antibiotics.

MRSA

Most harmful strains of Staphylococcus aureus (SA) are killed by the antibiotic methicillin, but some strains are unaffected. They are methicillin-resistant SA (MRSA), or superbugs.

WASH YOUR HANDS, PLEASE

Hospitals are full of sick people, many with bacterial and other microbial infections. It is easy to spread microbes accidentally by touching door handles, beds, chairs, and other items. Doctors, nurses, and visitors are encouraged to use antiseptic handwashes as often as possible.

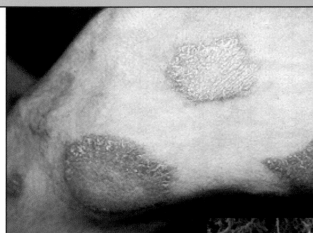

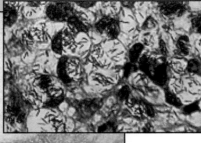

LEPROSY

For centuries Hansen's disease, or leprosy, was incurable, causing skin sores and other problems (left). Since the 1940s, medical drugs have been developed against the Mycobacterium leprae (above) that cause it.

DEADLY KILLERS

The body's white blood cells do not stay in the blood. In their search for bacteria to kill and eat, they squeeze out of blood vessels and roam among the tissues and organs.

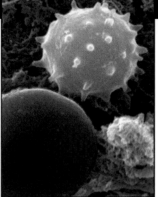

TESTING MRSA

MRSA bacteria (left) are grown in laboratories on agar gels. Each gel contains a certain kind of antibiotic. The gel where the bacteria do not grow has the antibiotic that works against that strain of MRSA superbug.

VACCINES

Vaccines are substances that build up the body's immunity, or resistance, to microbes. They are given to prevent bacterial diseases such as tetanus, typhoid, and anthrax.

SPREADING DISEASES

Some diseases are common only in certain areas. People living in these areas gradually build up a resistance. But if the disease spreads to a new area, the people there have little resistance and may die. This has happened over the centuries as explorers and settlers spread bacterial infections like pneumonia and syphilis.

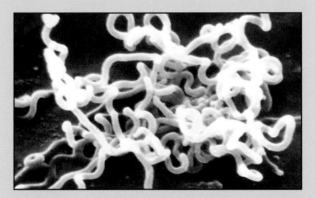

Treponema pallidum, *the cause of syphilis*

RESISTANCE

Sometimes when bacteria multiply, their DNA is not copied exactly. The result is a changed gene called a mutation. The mutation may be harmful and kill the bacteria. Or it may help the bacteria to resist an antibiotic drug. Then researchers have to develop a new kind of antibiotic.

BACTERIA AND VIRUSES

Bacteria are small, but viruses are far tinier. While many kinds of bacteria are either helpful or simply not harmful, all viruses are disease-causing because of the way they multiply.

ALL ABOUT VIRUSES

Viruses do not belong to any of the five kingdoms, but they are most commonly compared to bacteria. Most kinds of viruses are between one-tenth and one one-hundredth the size of an average bacterium. They are too small to see through a light microscope, and some can only be seen using an electron microscope. Various kinds of viruses are shaped like balls, boxes, pyramids, rods, golf balls, and tiny spaceships.

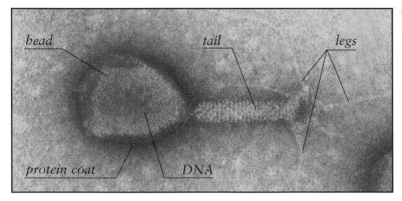

head · tail · legs · protein coat · DNA

T4 VIRUS

The T4 virus is a bacteriophage, which means it infects bacterial cells and multiplies inside them. It has an outer coat of protein subunits joined like building bricks, with a tail and long, thin "legs." Inside the head is the DNA.

ARE THEY ALIVE?

Viruses cannot move around or feed. They can only multiply inside another living cell. The virus gets inside and takes over the cell's processes to make more copies of itself, sometimes many thousands. This kills the cell. It then bursts open to release the viruses, which can then infect more cells.

MEASLES

Viral diseases include measles (right), as well as colds, mumps, rubella (German measles), polio, rabies, yellow fever, hepatitis, and types of meningitis.

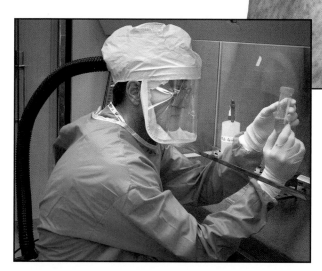

TAKING CARE

Like bacteria, viruses must be handled with extreme care in the laboratory. Also as with bacteria, their genetic material may change and create new strains. This is why people keep catching common colds and the flu.

PRIONS

Smaller than many viruses, prions have no DNA or other genetic material. They are made only of protein substances folded into a tangled-looking knot. Prions are thought to cause infections of the brain and nerves. Such diseases include bovine spongiform encephalopathy (mad cow disease) and Creutzfeldt-Jakob disease.

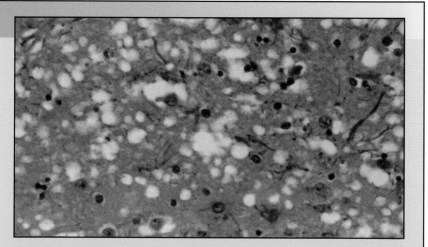

A microscope view of a cow's brain affected by BSE shows how it becomes swollen or inflamed and filled with holes like a sponge.

CLASSIFICATION OF LIFE

Scientists classify, or sort, living things depending on their features and the parts inside them that are similar to those of other living things. In microscopic life-forms of one cell each, these parts are very tiny. But they are important, because many of them are found in the cells of much larger living things, such as plants and animals. The single-celled bacteria and other microbes give us clues about how life on Earth started billions of years ago.

The main groups of living things are known as domains. The next divisions are usually kingdom, phylum, class, order, family, genus, and species. To see how this system works, follow the example of how the bacterium *Pseudomonas* is classified in the domain Bacteria.

THE DOMAINS OF LIFE

BACTERIA

 Single-celled prokaryotes, found in most places on Earth

ARCHAEA

 Single-celled prokaryotes, many surviving in extreme conditions

EUKARYA

KINGDOMS

 PROTISTA: Single-celled eukaryotes, with some simple multicelled forms

 FUNGI: Multicelled life-forms that digest their food externally

 PLANTAE: Multicelled life-forms obtaining energy by photosynthesis

ANIMALIA: Multicelled life-forms that get their energy by taking in food

GROUPS OF BACTERIA

Some experts estimate that there are about 10 major phyla of bacteria, while others suggest there are more than 50. Only a selection can be shown here.

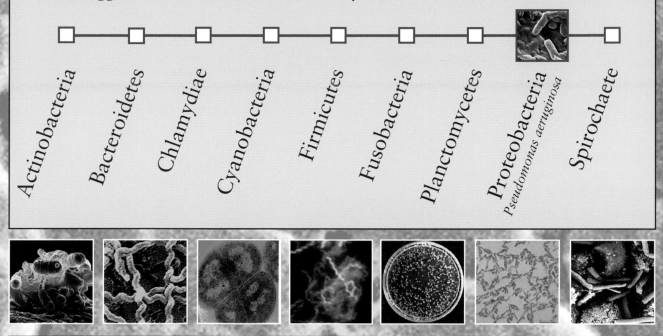

Actinobacteria

Bacteroidetes

Chlamydiae

Cyanobacteria

Firmicutes

Fusobacteria

Planctomycetes

Proteobacteria
Pseudomonas aeruginosa

Spirochaete

One of the most numerous types of bacterium is *Pseudomonas*. It is well-known from laboratory and genetic experiments as well as for causing diseases.

DOMAIN: Bacteria

PHYLUM: Proteobacteria

CLASS: Gamma Protebacteria

ORDER: Pseudomonadales

FAMILY: Pseudomonadales

GENUS: *Pseudomonas*

SPECIES: *aeruginosa*

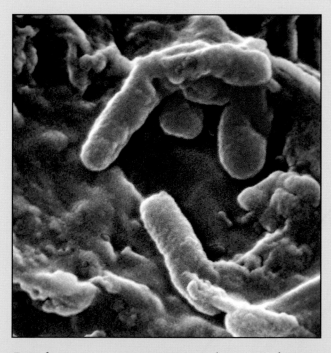

Pseudomonas aeruginosa causes human infections.

GLOSSARY

ACIDOPHILE
Living thing that can survive in extremely acidic conditions, such as a peat swamp

ANTIBIOTICS
Medical drugs that attack and disable or kill bacteria and similar microbe germs (but usually not viruses)

BACTERIOPHAGE
Virus that multiplies by getting into and taking over a bacterial cell

BIOLUMINESCENCE
The ability of living things to create light and shine or glow in the dark; caused by bacteria

CELL
Basic unit or "building block" of life; some microscopic living things, such as bacteria, have just one cell, while larger plants and animals are made of billions of cells

CELL MEMBRANE
Thin covering or "skin" of a living cell, such as a bacterium

CELL WALL
Thick outer layer of some cells, which gives the cell shape and strength

CHEMOTROPH
Living thing that gains energy from simple chemical substances (rather than from more complicated substances in food) or from light

CHLOROPLAST
Tiny part inside a living cell that contains the substances needed to capture light energy and carry out photosynthesis

CONJUGATION
Passing of DNA directly between two nearby microbes, such as bacteria

CULTURE
Growing bacteria and similar microbes in controlled conditions in a laboratory or similar place; often occurs with the use of petri dishes

CYTOPLASM
The watery fluid inside a cell in which various parts float and many substances are dissolved

DNA
Deoxyribonucleic acid, the chemical substance that carries genetic information about how a living thing grows and survives

EUKARYOTE
Living cell that has an outer cell membrane and other membranes inside; the membrane encloses parts of the cell, such as the nucleus

FLAGELLUM
Long, hairlike part that sticks out of a cell like a whip, which can be be waved or twirled around for movement

HALOPHILE
Living thing that can survive in very salty conditions, such as salt lakes

MITOCHONDRIA
Tiny, sausage-shaped parts inside a cell that break nutrients apart from food to get energy

PATHOGEN
Living thing that can cause a disease or illness

PETRI DISH
Round, shallow dish with a lid, usually made of clear plastic or glass; used for growing microbes, such as bacteria, and other tiny life-forms in controlled conditions

PILUS
Long, thin, tubelike part sticking out from a bacterium; used for exchanging genetic material

PHOTOSYNTHESIS
Process of trapping light energy in order to join simple substances to create food, which is used to grow, develop, and carry out life processes

PLASMID
Short length of genetic material in a living cell that is in addition to the main lengths, or chromosomes, of DNA

PROKARYOTE
Living cell that has a cell membrane covering but no separate membranes inside; it lacks membrane-enclosed parts, such as a nucleus

RIBOSOMES
Ball-shaped parts inside a living thing that build its structural substances, known as proteins

SYMBIOSIS
When two very different kinds or species of living things exist very closely together, and both benefit from the partnership

THERMOPHILE
Living thing that can survive in very hot conditions, such as superheated mineral springs

VACUOLE
Pool or blob of a substance inside a living cell, such as water, nutrients, or waste products

XEROPHILE
Living thing that can survive in very dry conditions, such as a desert

Look for all the books in this series:

FURTHER RESOURCES

FURTHER READING
Brunelle, Lynn, and Barbara Ravage, eds. *Bacteria*. Gareth Stevens Publishing, 2003.

Favor, Lesli J. *Bacteria*. Rosen Publishing, 2003.

Snedden, Robert. *The Benefits of Bacteria*. Chicago: Heinemann Library, 2007.

Stewart, Melissa. *Classification of Life*. Minneapolis: Twenty-First Century Books, 2008.

INTERNET SITES
FactHound offers a safe, fun way to find Internet sites related to this book. All of the sites on FactHound have been researched by our staff.

Here's all you do:

Visit *www.facthound.com*

FactHound will fetch the best sites for you!

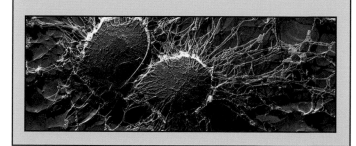

INDEX